HOW? WHO? WHAT? WHEN? WHERE? WHY?

Questions Kids ask

ABOUT
TOYS, GAMES AND SPORTS

PUBLISHER	Joseph R. DeVarennes	
PUBLICATION DIRECTOR	Kenneth H. Pearson	
ADVISORS	Roger Aubin	
	Robert Furlonger	
EDITORIAL SUPERVISOR	Jocelyn Smyth	
PRODUCTION MANAGER	Ernest Homewood	
PRODUCTION ASSISTANTS	Martine Gingras	Kathy Kishimoto
	Catherine Gordon	Peter Thomlison
CONTRIBUTORS	Alison Dickie	Nancy Prasad
	Bill Ivy	Lois Rock
	Jacqueline Kendel	Merebeth Switzer
	Anne Langdon	Dave Taylor
	Sheila Macdonald	Alison Tharen
	Susan Marshall	Donna Thomson
	Pamela Martin	Pam Young
	Colin McCance	
SENIOR EDITOR	Robin Rivers	
EDITORS	Brian Cross	Ann Martin
	Anne Louise Mahoney	Mayta Tannenbaum
PUBLICATION ADMINISTRATOR	Anna Good	
ART AND DESIGN	Richard Comely	Ronald Migliore
	George Elliott	Sue Wilkinson
	Greg Elliott	

Canadian Cataloguing in Publication Data

Main entry under title:

Questions kids ask about toys, games and sports

(Questions kids ask ; 4)
ISBN 0-7172-2543-7

1. Toys—Miscellanea—Juvenile literature.   2. Games—Miscellanea—
Juvenile literature.   3. Sports—Miscellanea—Juvenile literature.
4. Children's questions and answers.
I. Smyth, Jocelyn.   II. Comely, Richard.   III. Series.

GV1203.Q48 1988   j790.1'922   C89-093158-5

Questions Kids Ask . . . about TOYS, GAMES AND SPORTS

continued

How do surfers stay on their boards?

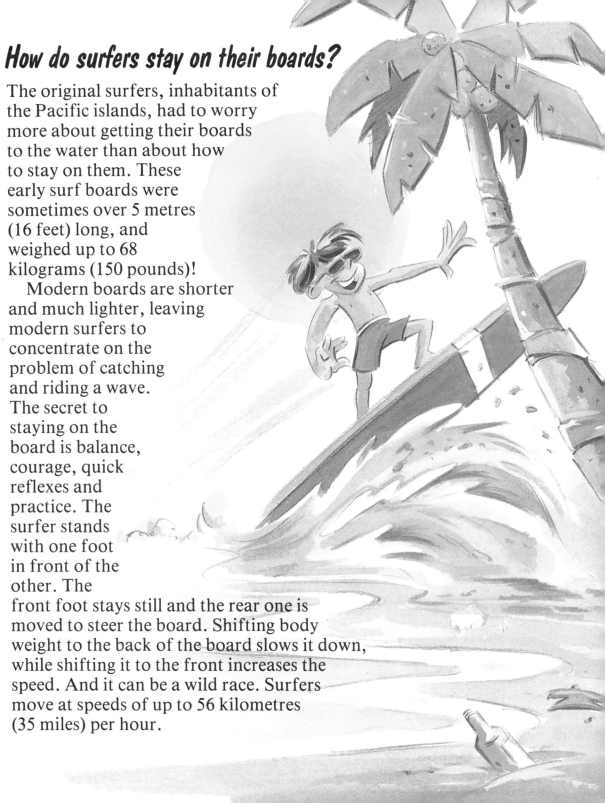

The original surfers, inhabitants of the Pacific islands, had to worry more about getting their boards to the water than about how to stay on them. These early surf boards were sometimes over 5 metres (16 feet) long, and weighed up to 68 kilograms (150 pounds)!

Modern boards are shorter and much lighter, leaving modern surfers to concentrate on the problem of catching and riding a wave. The secret to staying on the board is balance, courage, quick reflexes and practice. The surfer stands with one foot in front of the other. The front foot stays still and the rear one is moved to steer the board. Shifting body weight to the back of the board slows it down, while shifting it to the front increases the speed. And it can be a wild race. Surfers move at speeds of up to 56 kilometres (35 miles) per hour.

What is the world's most popular board game?

In 1933 an unemployed heating engineer named Charles Darrow invented a real estate game called Monopoly. He sold it to Parker Brothers in 1935, and soon Monopoly was the best-selling game in the world. To this day it is still the most popular board game.

Since 1935 Parker Brothers has sold more than 10 million sets! Editions of the game are published in 27 countries and printed in 15 different languages.

The first Monopoly game was printed on an oil cloth. The houses and hotels were cut from scraps of wood and colored buttons were used for the playing pieces. The streets were named after real streets in Atlantic City, New Jersey, where Darrow and his family spent their vacations. Today some editions use the street names of the country the game will be sold in. In Britain, for example, the game uses street names taken from the city of London.

DID YOU KNOW . . . Parker Brothers prints about $18 500 000 000 000 (that's $18.5 TRILLION) worth of Monopoly play money every year!

How fast do downhill skiers go?

The skiers who race for the World Cup go down the sides of the mountains at speeds that can hit 160 kilometres (100 miles) an hour. However, a downhill ski course has many slower sections in it, so the average speed is about half of that.

Downhill racing is one of the most demanding of all sports. Often the difference between winning and placing fifth is only a few one-hundredths of a second. World Cup skiers are highly skilled and have worked very hard for many years, yet they can still lose by an amount of time most of us can't even measure.

What is a hockey puck made of?

In earlier times hockey was played with pucks made of all kinds of things. You may have played hockey using a rubber ball as a puck. But the official modern hockey puck is a disk that is 2.54 centimetres (1 inch) thick and 7.62 centimetres (3 inches) in diameter and that weighs between 156 and 170 grams (5.5–6 ounces). It is made of black vulcanized rubber. Vulcanization is a process that makes rubber stronger and allows it to keep its elasticity over a greater temperature range. That means that the puck won't freeze during the game and stop bouncing off the boards.

Why do referees wear black and white striped shirts?

Referees haven't always worn black and white striped shirts. In the late 1930s, all referees' shirts were solid white. In the late 1940s, they were bright orange, then for a while white again. But this all changed in 1954 when sporting event organizers began getting ready for television.

Black and white vertical stripes stand out better than any other colors or patterns on a black and white television screen. Referees were given black and white vertical striped shirts to wear so that the TV viewers could easily tell them from the players. The tradition has stuck, and referees still wear black and white striped shirts, even on color TV.

Who is the tallest basketball player in the world?

Can you imagine what it would be like to be 2.45 metres (8 feet) tall? That's the height of the tallest basketball player, Suleinan Ali Nashnush. He played for the Lybian Basketball Team in 1963.

How fast can the fastest racing car go?

In 1979, an American driver named Stan Barrett drove a rocket-engined racing car, at an incredible 1190 kilometres (739 miles) per hour. Although it wasn't during an official race, it is the fastest car speed ever recorded. It's more than ten times the speed that we drive on the highways.

DID YOU KNOW . . . the first organized car race was held in Paris, France, in 1894. The average speed of the winning car was 18.7 kilometres (11.6 miles) per hour.

9

What is hang gliding?

Have you ever flown a kite? If you have, then you will know that the wind can catch and carry a kite high into the sky. A hang glider is very much like a big kite with a place for a person to ride attached underneath it.

A hang glider usually takes off from clifftops or hills, or is towed along the water by a motor boat to get it into the air. Once it is up, the pilot hangs from a harness and steers the glider with a control bar that shifts its frame. The glider sails through the sky— almost like a sailboat floats across the water. That is why hang gliding is sometimes called sky surfing.

How does a kite fly?

You know that you need a windy day to fly a kite. You have to get the kite far enough off the ground that the wind gets caught under it. Then what happens is that the force of the wind pushes the kite up into the air. You have to make sure, though, that the kite is tilted at the right angle to be lifted up, or the wind can blow it back down to the ground.

Kites can have many different shapes. Often they are made to look like fantastic birds or animals. But however they are shaped, they are designed to hold the air like a sail, so they can ride the wind up into the sky.

What is skydiving?

You may have seen people on TV jumping out of a plane and falling throught the air with huge grins on their faces. They are enjoying the thrill of free fall.

Free fall is part of the daredevil sport of skydiving. The jumper is in free fall after leaving the plane and before opening the chute. After leaving the plane the jumper moves his or her body to stay in balance and to get into position over a landing target. Then the chute is opened and, if the position is right, the skydiver drifts slowly down to land right on target.

Why do golf balls have dimples?

If you stuffed a small bull hide bag full of feathers, do you think you could hit it very far with a golf club? Well, it wouldn't fly any distance and the ball would quickly lose its shape. But the feathery, as this ball was known, was the most popular golf ball 150 years ago!

Then someone created a nearly indestructible ball out of the juice of a gutta-percha tree. It flew much farther than the feathery. The only problem with the new gold ball was that it quickly dropped out of the air because of its smooth surface. Someone came up with the great idea of making small circular dents, or

dimples, on the surface. This made the ball fly more smoothly.

Nowadays golf balls are wound with rubber. The dimples are arranged in various patterns to make the balls fly higher, lower or farther. This helps the golfer to have more control over where it goes. So all those little dimples are very important.

DID YOU KNOW . . . the average golf ball has 384 dimples!

What makes a baseball curve?

The first major league pitcher to throw a curveball was Fred Goldsmith who played for the Guelph Maple Leafs in 1874. Since then the curveball has become one of the standard pitches in baseball.

To throw a curveball the pitcher holds the ball off-center and throws it with a snap and a

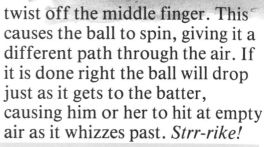

twist off the middle finger. This causes the ball to spin, giving it a different path through the air. If it is done right the ball will drop just as it gets to the batter, causing him or her to hit at empty air as it whizzes past. *Strr-rike!*

DID YOU KNOW . . . a curveball is also called a "jug," "rainbow," "dipsy-do," "hook" and "snake."

What was the longest sailing race?

People have probably been racing for as long as they have been sailing, but the first official international race was held in 1851. Called the Hundred Guineas Cup, it was a race across the Atlantic from North America to England and then around the Isle of Wight. It was won by the *America,* whose owners returned the cup to be the prize in future races of what is now the most famous international competition, the America's Cup.

The course of this race is now just a race around the Isle of Wight, and so it is far from being the longest race. The longest race ever sailed was from San Francisco, California, to Papeete, Tahiti, 3687 nautical miles (approximately 6831 kilometres, or 4240 miles). It was sailed in 1925 and won by L.A. Norris's *Mariner.*

How can a sailboat sail into the wind?

If a sailboat headed directly into the wind the sails would flap and the boat would stop moving forward. Instead sailboats sail across the wind, doing something called "beating." This way they can zig-zag, or tack, ahead in the direction they want to go in, in spite of the direction of the wind. The sailor positions the boat and the sails so that the wind coming at it will pull it forward at an angle. When the boat has gone a certain distance, the sailor angles off in the opposite direction. That way the sailboat continues moving forward without going too far out of the way.

Can a boat sail on ice?

If speed is what you like, you'll like sailing on ice better than on water. Ice boats of different sizes and shapes have been around for a long time. The common ones today are simply three runners mounted on a triangular frame that has a single mast with one or two sails. This simple boat will go at incredible speeds. The official record is 230 kilometres (143 miles) per hour, but unofficially ice boats have been clocked at 257 kilometres (160 miles) per hour.

DID YOU KNOW . . . you can sail on ice without a boat! Skate sailors wear long-bladed racing skates and carry a frame covered with a sail on one shoulder. They can reach speeds of up to 100 kilometres (60 miles) an hour.

Who invented roller skates?

James Plimpton of Massachusetts invented roller skates and patented them in 1863. But there were others before him who tried something similar.

Legend has it that the first roller skater was a 17th-century Dutchman who attached wooden rollers to his skates. But he was apparently the only one who did, and it was a hundred years before another roller skater turned up.

In 1760 a Belgian musician named Joseph Merlin attached metal wheels to the bottom of his shoes. He thought he was really on to something and decided to stage a demonstration at a party. He skated through the room playing his violin, and everything

went smoothly until he realized that he couldn't stop. He crashed into a large mirror, smashing it and his violin and his head. Ouch! No more roller skating for another 89 years. This time, the roller skates, shoes with metal wheels, were used at the Paris Opera House in an opera that had an ice skating scene. The roller skates were a success and they became a big fad in France and England. But it wasn't until James Plimpton's skates that the world had roller skates that allowed the skater to turn!

What is a unicycle?

Do you know what a tricycle is? Of course you do: it's something you ride around on that has three wheels. But even if you had never seen a tricycle, the word would give you a clue to what it is because *tri* means three. *Bi* means two, so a bicycle is a cycle with two wheels. *Uni* means one. Now can you guess what a unicycle is? A unicycle is a cycle with one wheel, of course.

The pedals of a unicycle are attached to the one wheel in much the same way that the pedals of a tricycle are attached to its front wheel. The seat of the unicycle is on top of forks also attached to the wheel. There are no handlebars.

If you think that unicycles must be difficult to ride, you're right! But they can be ridden after lots of practice, and some people are very good at riding them.

DID YOU KNOW . . . a bicycle built for two is called a "tandem."

What race gives a cowbell for first prize?

The oldest motorcycle race in North America is the Jack Pine Enduro, first held on September 1, 1923, and still run every Labor Day in Lansing, Michigan.

Back in the early years of the race, the course wasn't as well marked as it is today, and one year a group of racers got sidetracked into a cow pasture. One of the riders found a cow bell and carried it with him for the rest of the race. He presented it to the winner as a joke, and the joke stuck. Since that time, the winner of the Jack Pine Enduro is awarded an engraved copper cowbell for a trophy!

Why do track bicycle racers wear gloves?

You would think all bicycles must have brakes, otherwise how would they stop? But the bicycles used for track racing are built *without* brakes.

A track racing bicycle is stripped to only essential parts to keep its weight as low as possible. Extra weight slows the bike down. So how do you stop it? This is where the gloves come in. The racer back pedals, then reaches forward and grabs the front wheel. This stops the wheel spinning, and the bicycle comes to a stop. No wonder track bicycle racers wear gloves! If they didn't their hands would get terribly scraped every time they tried to stop.

What is a steeplechase?

Have you ever raced along a route that had different kinds of obstacles like logs and fences that had to be jumped over? If you have, then you've been in a steeplechase.

The first steeplechases were run on horseback in Ireland in the 18th century. They were run for fun by hunters riding home after fox-hunting. Since they were in open country, there were always obstacles to overcome such as streams, fences and large rocks. These races were called steeplechases because often a church steeple was used as the finish line since it could be seen from a long way away.

DID YOU KNOW . . . the steeplechase run on foot became an Olympic event in 1920.

20

What game was invented to replace war?

Chess is probably the oldest game known. Some people claim it is more than 500 years old! No one knows for sure who invented it, but it is generally believed to have originated in India and was first played by Buddhist monks. Buddhists are not allowed to fight wars because war involves killing. So they invented chess, a game which uses war-like strategy, as a substitute. The game spread to Persia, Arabia, and then to Western Europe. Unfortunately it hasn't replaced war.

What sport was used to train warriors for battle?

The first settlers to arrive in North America watched the Indians play a game they called "baggataway." The game was played in a large field with a ball and long crossed sticks. The sticks reminded the French settlers of a *crosse,* or bishop's staff, so they named the game "lacrosse."

Lacrosse is still a popular sport, but then it was more than just a game. The Iroquois prepared their warriors for battle by sending them to play lacrosse against a rival tribe. Sometimes there were as many as 500 on each team, and the game could last for days. It wasn't your usual friendly competitive game. The players used any tactic they could think of to win and broken bones were common. Lacrosse is still considered one of the fiercest and fastest of team sports.

Why does a rubber ball bounce?

Rubber is a very special material because it has high elasticity. This means that it can be stretched to many times its natural length and still spring back to its original shape when it is released.

This elasticity is what makes a rubber ball bounce. When you throw it against the ground, the side that hits is flattened by the force of the throw. But the rubber springs back to its original round shape and so is pushed up off the ground again. This is why a rubber ball will bounce higher the harder you throw it down.

What makes a boomerang come back?

It's all in how you throw it! Well, it's in the shape of the boomerang too. Not all boomerangs are meant to come back. Some are used for hunting, and are just thrown to hit and kill an animal. But the returning boomerang is special. It is a stick with two arms at an angle of at least 90 degrees. The arms are twisted slightly, as if you had held the boomerang by its tips and twisted just a little bit. One side of the boomerang is flat, the other is slightly rounded. The flat side and curved side give the boomerang life, like the wings of

an airplane lift it. The twist that the whole thing has makes it turn.

To throw the boomerang you hold it vertically and throw it with a spinning motion. It will go straight and then turn to the horizontal and start to rise in the air. Then the boomerang will turn to the left (if it is thrown with the right hand, otherwise it will turn to the right) and come around back to the thrower.

When was soccer invented?

Soccer is a very old game. There is a record of a soccer-like game being played in the Orient in 1004 B.C., and we know that the ancient Greeks and Romans played. The game was introduced to the rest of Europe by the Romans when they were building their empire. But soccer was not then—nor for centuries—what it is like now. There were almost no rules and a game could go on for days, ending up in a brawl far from where it started.

In the 19th century, private schools in England developed rules for the game, and since then it has changed little. Today, the brawling is done by the fans of this, the most popular of team sports.

DID YOU KNOW . . . soccer stadiums are the largest sports arenas in the world, holding crowds of up to 200 000 people. The largest is in Rio de Janeiro, Brazil.

What sport uses the largest ball?

In England there is a field game called earthball that uses the largest ball of any sport. It has almost no rules and is played by any number of people divided into two teams. An earthball measures a couple of metres (over 6 feet) in diameter.

The game is played by placing the huge ball in the middle of a field 183 by 137 metres (200 by 150 yards). Then the teams run toward the ball and try to kick it through the other team's goal posts. The game ends when the players decide they have had enough. The team with most points at that time is declared the winner.

What sport is played on the largest field?

Polo, a ball game played on horseback, is played on a field 274 metres (300 yards) long by 183 metres (200 yards) wide. Sometimes the sidelines are boarded, in which case the field is reduced to 146 metres (160 yards) wide. In polo, two teams of four players try to hit a ball with mallets through the other team's goal posts while riding horses. With eight horses galloping at full speed, you can see why polo needs such a large field!

Who invented the yo-yo?

"Yo-yo" is the trade name of a toy introduced into the United States by Donald F. Duncan, after he saw Filipino immigrants on the docks of San Francisco playing with something similar. But the yo-yo, also known as a returning top, is a toy that has been around for a long time and turns up in many different places. It is thought that it originated in China. In 18th-century England there was a returning top known as the quiz or the Prince of Wales top. At that time there was also a similar toy in France known as a *bandalore*. Why not get a yo-yo and try going around-the-world yourself?

How did the teddy bear get its name?

Most children in North America have owned a teddy bear. Teddy bears have been a favorite stuffed toy for many years, and toymakers around the world still make thousands of them every year.

The teddy bear is named for Theodore (Teddy) Roosevelt, the very popular president of the United States from 1901 to 1909. The story goes that he rescued a black bear cub that was about to be killed by a hunter. The incident prompted a toymaker to make a stuffed bear toy and call it the teddy bear. The new toy was very popular, and the rest, as they say, is history.

When were the first playing cards used?

A deck of 52 cards like the one we use today was first created in France, but there were playing cards in the world long before that. The modern deck was created by combining two earlier decks, one with just numbered cards and the Tarot, a deck with just picture cards. The new deck was divided into four suits which were distinguished by different markings: a clover leaf, a spear tip, a heart and a diamond. These came to be called in English by the familiar names club, spade, heart and diamond.

DID YOU KNOW . . . there were playing cards in China a thousand years ago.

How do you juggle?

You've probably seen jugglers at the circus tossing and catching hoops, balls, bottles or even china plates. You hold your breath as they throw as many as 10 or 12 high into the air, thinking that surely they'll drop one. But they don't!

Juggling may look like magic, but it really isn't. It's just a matter of practice. You could start with a couple of oranges, or something else that is easy to catch and throw and won't break if dropped. Take an orange in each hand. First throw the orange in one hand, then the one in the other, not too high, and catch them in the opposite hands. Practice this until you can do it smoothly without dropping them and without moving your arms around too wildly. Then add a third.

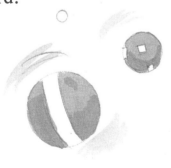

Start again, this time with two oranges in one hand and one in the other. And practice, practice, practice. Soon they'll be going around in a nice smooth arc and you'll be ready to add more and more. But if you never get up to 12 don't be too upset. The jugglers in the circus practice for years and sometimes they make a mistake. And when they do . . . *crash!*

Who made the first doll?

Dolls have been around for many thousands of years. Although we usually think of dolls as toys, the first dolls we know of were not toys at all.

The earliest dolls known were found in Egyptian graves dating back about 4000 years. They were wooden carvings called "paddle dolls" because they were made from a flat piece of wood shaped like a paddle. After the figure was carved, clothes were painted on and strings of clay beads were attached to its head to look like hair or a headdress. Egyptians thought that placing the dolls in someone's grave would provide the person with servants in the next world.

The first dolls known to be toys date back to ancient Greece. These dolls had moveable arms and legs. Girls played with dolls until they got married, then they left them on the altar of the goddess Artemis to show they had outgrown childish things.

How can a fly catch a fish?

Flies don't catch fish! Fish catch flies. Don't they? Sure they do. But sometimes a fish catches a fly that catches the fish for a fisherman, called an angler. People have been catching fish with flies for more than 2000 years. It was observed that some fish feed on flies on or near the surface of the water. So someone came up with the idea of putting a hook in a fly and placing it at the surface of the water to catch the fish. Unfortunately, getting real insects onto a hook can be a problem, so the art of artificial fly making was born. An angler from the third century described the artificial fly he made from red wool and two feathers from the neck of a chicken.

How do divers know where the water is?

If you stand high above a pool of water or a lake that is perfectly calm and still, you will have trouble seeing exactly where the air stops and the water starts. Competition divers have to be able to time their entry into the water perfectly in order to do it properly. So a hose is sprayed on the water, causing it to ripple and allowing the diver to see exactly where the surface is.

Why do we call the center of a target the "bull's eye"?

Objects are often named after things that they have something in common with. The center of a blown sheet of glass is called a bull's-eye because it is round, thick and slightly curved like the eye of a bull. The bull's-eye on a target is not thicker than the rest of the target, nor is it curved, but it is in the center, and it is round. So it is something like the bull's-eye on a sheet of glass, even though it isn't much like the eye of a bull.

You've probably heard people say "Bull's-eye!" meaning that's exactly right. This is nothing like the eye of a bull, but being exactly right is like hitting the bull's-eye on a target. So you can see how one word, "bull's-eye," can come to mean many different things.

31

Index _____